Life Lies

The cultivation of sacrifice to success
from a broken king's journey

CHA-CHI SIMMONS
CO-WRITER: DARRIN CAMPBELL

DISCLAIMER

The advice contained in this material might not be suitable for everyone. The author designed the information to present his opinion about the subject matter. The reader must carefully investigate all aspects of any life decision before committing him or herself. The author obtained the information contained herein from sources he believes to be reliable and from his own personal experience, but he neither implies nor intends any guarantee of accuracy. The author is not in the business of giving legal, counseling, or any other type of professional advice. Should the reader need such advice, he or she must seek services from a competent professional. The author particularly disclaims any liability, loss, or risk taken by individuals who directly or indirectly act on the information contained herein. The author believes the advice presented here is sound, but readers cannot hold him responsible for either the actions they take, or the risk taken by individuals who directly or indirectly act on the information contained herein. Although the author and publisher have made every effort to ensure that the information in this book was correct at press time, the author and publisher do not assume and hereby disclaim any liability to any party for any loss, damage, or disruption caused by errors or omissions, whether such errors or omissions result from negligence, accident, or any other cause.

Published by Cheno Publishing LLC
Copyright © 2020 by Cheno Publishing LLC

ISBN: 978-1-7354510-1-5 (eBook)
ISBN: 978-1-7354510-0-8 (Paperback)

Cover Photo Copyright © 2020 by Cheno Publishing LLC
Cover Photo and author photo shot by Kyler Ledee
Cover design and book formatting by Rica Cabrex
Editing by Krystal Chevis

"We will never witness real peace and overstanding until we can master endorsing each other's greatness."

"Finding yourself in seemingly frivolous conditions has an accumulative purpose; one that is not recognized until your final destination."

—Cha-Chi Simmons

Cha-Chi & Cheno

"They tried to bury us, they didn't know we were seeds."

—*Dinos Christianopoulos*

CONTENTS

DEDICATION

Yahweh Elohim, you have allowed me to experience every pain, every version of anger, every version of ostracization, every version of neglect, just so that I have the experience and qualification to be the author of this book. Although I will never understand the totality of your thinking, I do know that there is nothing on this earth, in this existence, that was not created by you and from you; whether it be pain, anger, or even fear. So I thank you for loving me enough to equip me with these emotional tools and these various versions of mental machinery so that I could maintain the strength to keep the promise that I made, to remain a fragrance instead of an odor, throughout my existence in this world. Thank you.

This book is dedicated to everyone that has suffered for me to grow. To my mom, Mary Lois Guidry, and my step-father Wilson Guidry, as well as my biological dad, because it is the trepidation and the chaos, the detriments, the blood, and the sirens that your acquaintance suffered, which caused me to suffer. But it's okay. Thank you, because now that suffering has blessed the world and become a lesson of self-preservation, a blueprint for success and survival. Thank you.

To K-Dog, the guy whose life I took, as a boy. I made a promise to you since your death, that together we would become Kings and we would fix our community. You live through me now, so your soul can rest in confidence. Obviously, neither one of us had ever truly known love, but together we will love and love eternally. You sacrificed so that we could bless the world with the experience and the knowledge that I have gained from your death. I promised you that you will live on forever. You will live on, associated with the true definition of love, LUV, love with the "u". That "u" begins the word "US," my brother. Rest easy and in honor. Rest easy my brother, because in your death you have become God. One Luv.

To my young trees, my children: Shana, Marquis, Brooklyn, Alex, Macho, and Oriyah, we adapted, adopted, and arose. WE DID IT!

To my grand babies Ma'layah, Keani and Camie, Papa had you in mind long before your introduction to this sewage called life. Every ounce of suffering that we have incurred was worth the lesson so that you could elude the horrors which are plagued on the Simmons' blood. You will experience a luxury that none of us Simmons has ever felt before. True freedom!!

Lastly, this is dedicated to all the people who have antagonized my auspiciousness, who have dedicated their lives to turn everything that was good in me, as a youth and adult, into a war. May Yahweh bless you because the tactics that I have learned in that war has become my power, my energy, my momentum and now I also fight in my sleep. Even in my ignorance I will continue to fight, even in my unconsciousness. That fight is called positivity, winning. To those who said they loved me, who said they'd die for me; I realized that you couldn't even live for me. You left me in prison to die and for that attempted abortion, I thank you. I really appreciate it because I needed that. Today what I used to call regrets, have been replaced with knowledge.

ACKNOWLEDGEMENTS

To my mom, Mary Lois August Simmons Guidry, otherwise known as Cheno. Although your physicalness has gone back home to the Almighty, I know that your mission to protect and provide for your baby boy has not ended. In your youth, you willingly suffered the plague of bullets riddling your body, to protect me. You lived a life of torture from paralysis and suffering from utter pain and confusion. You fought mental wars, physical wars, as well as emotional wars. And as I stated previously, you WILLINGLY did that for me and my brothers and sisters. You kept the promise that you made to yourself, to love beyond condition, the seeds, the young trees that you brought into this world. Due to excruciating circumstances and situations, I know that you were limited in your capabilities, limited in your abilities to make sound decisions. However, you did everything that you were supposed to. You equipped me, and us, with everything we needed to be leaders, conquerors of this behemoth called life. As long as I live, my goal is to continue to keep the promise, which was to never make you cry over me again, and to be the path for those of our bloodline navigating behind me. For those that choose the path of progression, I will remain that example, and I will always have that avenue open for those with the will to escape the trepidation that comes with being a Simmons. I am keeping that promise in your name, Cheno. I luv you and thank you for being mighty, for being my God, and my example of strength.

Krystal Chevis, my divine empress, you walked into my life when my world was being ravished with earthquakes, tornadoes, and thunderstorms. You recognized that my life was hanging on by a straw and I would not survive that Armageddon; none the less, you willingly walked into that war with no intentions other than to help save my life. You are the definition of beauty. You are the definition of luv. True example of queen and lady. I will luv you until my last, last breath. In previous relationships I have had to witness the black woman with the misguided perception of where she should stand when joining the war that her king, the black man, has found himself in. Instead of standing face-to-face with me in the middle of my war, without me saying so, you took your place standing shoulder to shoulder, prepared to battle side by side. Sometimes even a step behind me, where you were prepared to push when I pushed. You understood that face-to-face would only have you either in my way or have yourself in danger with your back turned to the enemy. Your wisdom and your foresight has preserved me and helped to shape me into the king that I am today. I have always had the strength of a lion, and the power of an ox. However, amidst the normalcy of these two strengths battling one another, you helped me to recognize that organizing the two powers and using them for righteousness would earn me my crown. Your loyalty has created in me a pillar, and true prophet.

Darrin Campbell, through you, I have had the opportunity to witness a disciple on Earth. Since knowing you, it has been a pleasure of mine, (while this race issue is a pandemic of its own) to be able to tell people that I know a white man who overstands the true definition of luv, with overstanding of the true definition of life. A white man who grasps the purpose of togetherness and teamwork and gives a face to the existence of the two. Side by side, we persevere in our quest to create a world where young people can recognize that they are created in the image of the Almighty; the image of man himself, the image of a king despite race, despite their tribulations. You are a powerful man, and sometimes I think the term man is an understatement when referring to you my brother. In this instance, we share the true definition and the true spelling of the word luv. We both spell luv with a "u" and that "u" begins the word "US" my brother. Thank you for holding me up in my moments of challenge. Thank you for being my homie and being able to be honest with me, being able to luv this black man without an ulterior motive. Thank you for exercising true overstanding with me and the troubled youth of our society. One luv.

To Kyler, the cover photo is amazing! Thanks for your auspiciousness in just wanting to see me rise. With your photography skills, you've managed to capture the true essence of my feelings. You demonstrate the true definition of being your brother's keeper. THANK YOU!!!

Darrin Campbell, Krystal Chevis, you have helped me to keep the promise of creating this book. I could not have accomplished this feat without your contributions. Words cannot express my thoughts and appreciation. This product is the result of your patience, brilliance, and diligence. I LUV U BOTH!!

PREFACE

L ast - coming after all others in time or order; final.

What represents the definition of last, more than finding yourself a slave, unjustly, physically, mentally, and spiritually, in a 4 by 6 prison cell on a death row tier with concrete walls and steel doors in the bloodiest prison in the nation, where the only music you here is the beat of your heart and the rhythm of your breathing. Where the only friends you have are your guilt and your regrets.

First - coming before all others in time or order; earliest foremost in position, rank, or importance; principal.

What fits the definition of first better than becoming an educator, becoming a leader, becoming a savior, becoming a disciple, sacrificing all that you are and all that helped you to survive just to save and help fix the less fortunate, the unconscious, and the lost.

In this book you will learn that I have been last, and you will learn of my transition, the battle, the power, that I have developed inside of myself. You will learn about the sacrifices that I made for me to be able to wear the crown, the position of being first. You will see the evidence of how I recognized that I am no longer a lamb but a lion, a true king, a true leader, a true protector, a true prophet in this concrete jungle of struggles.

A MESSAGE FROM
THE CO-WRITER,
DARRIN CAMPBELL

I remember meeting Marcus years ago. I wish I could say that I saw him for who he is, the savior and king, immediately. I didn't. I saw the man covered in jailhouse tats, dressed in welding FR gear, and took him at face value. That lasted all of 30 seconds, though, because as soon as we had a conversation, I knew that I was working with a real teacher.

I've been a teacher for 17 years now. To be honest, all through university, I never wanted to be a teacher. I saw all the bullshit my mom had to suffer through during her teaching career, and I knew the money wasn't worth the headache and heartache. But damned if I didn't fall in love with the profession in grad school. The very first day I stood in front of a class, I knew I was at home. I wanted to help everyone, save everyone, push them to be better and pursue lives worth living. I've dedicated myself to this career thusly. In Marcus, I found a kindred spirit, one whose heartbeat to the same tune, one who would do anything in his power for his kids, those he sired and those in the desks.

Y'all consider this, now. I grew up in the middle of the woods in Sabine Parish, where nature still flourishes gorgeously, despite the rebel flags being as common as damn bath towels. There was a damn David Duke store down the road from where I lived when he was running for governor. If you don't know who David Duke is, look it up. Needless to say, racism and divisiveness prevailed. My parents always taught me right, though. They never lied to me, and they always encouraged me to make up my own damn mind.

Now, what are the chances of some good ol' boy from backwoods Louisiana meets up with a streetcat from Lafayette and they find so much in common? I feel that the good Lord had a plan for us, that we were meant to meet and write this book, to shout the message of this book for all the world to hear. Fate brought us together to do great things. We've saved many lives, hundreds if not thousands. We've turned people around from doomed walks of life towards careers, towards usefulness and prosperity. Sure, we didn't save everyone, but we sure as fuck never gave up trying.

I always make two promises to my students: I'll never lie to you, and I'll never give up on you. You, reading this, I'm making the same promises. Nothing in this book is a lie. And we, Marcus and I, will never give up on you. All of you can ascend. All of you can achieve greatness. All of you are Kings and Queens.

I'd like to thank Marcus for always being there for me, for being like a brother to me, and for trusting me to help him make this book a reality. I'd also like to thank my little girl, Cora, for showing me what strength is. At two months old, she had a coin flip's chance of surviving congestive heart failure. Today, you'd never know that beautiful little angel had to survive four surgeries, two on her heart, before she was two years old. Lastly, and most importantly, I want to thank my wife, Meghan. Baby, thank you so much for being my partner, my teammate, my soulmate. Thank you for my whole life. You made me the man I was always supposed to be. I love you!

Darrin Campbell

INTRODUCTION

I feel compelled to explain a few things before you navigate the following pages. Some words, phrases, and philosophies that I built, and that built me.

Growing up, the choice of idolizing drug pushers or Rasta men was too complicated as a kid. Because we needed a roof over our head and I needed guidance, I chose both. I only listened to Reggae music, and as life would have it, Reggae music became my father, nurturing my confusions and self-esteem. It taught me to stop judging myself and finding myself guilty of my stagnation. The language and self-reflection that I learned became a part of my culture. These teachings, along with my mom's, have prepared and guided me on my multiple tours of life's lies. Still today, I abide by these teachings and use the same methods to coach so many of the underserved youth through their versions of life's lies.

Overstanding means the ability to have foresight and see beyond your situation, or a particular situation. It is a maximum level of comprehension. "Understanding" implies that one would understand what's going on in the background and underneath everything. Overstanding, that's when you see the whole big picture, like a God's eye view. I learned the use of this word in my exposure to the Rastafarian teachings.

Within the prison walls, being labeled a convict is actually a compliment. It means that you have grown to be wise while doing time, as opposed to an inmate, who is just locked up, not learning anything, just aging.

Young tree is referring to the youth. Trees begin life as a helpless seed, just like babies. Like a seed, the youth need nurturing, they need conscious guidance. The amount of nurturing that it receives will determine how healthy the fruit they bear will be.

Yahweh is the true, and original name of the heavenly father, by which he chose for himself. Elohim is his title, like Lord or God. Yahshua is the original name of Jesus.

CHAPTER 1

Know Yourself

With everything that I've been through, I learned one irrefutable fact—I am strong, strong beyond measure. True strength isn't measured by strength of arms or how much damage you can inflict. It is measured by how much punishment you can take while you stay on your feet; how much you can endure and keep breathing; how much you can survive. My strength comes from my roots and how much the people that came before me, my forefathers and mothers, had to endure.

We, our ancestors, survived everything. We survived the belly of the ships, watching mothers and fathers whipped to ribbons, seeing babies used as bait to catch sharks. We survived being set on fire. We survived being raped. We survived being stabbed in the eyes for reading.

We survived hearing our brothers and sisters scream in pain as they were pulled apart by horses. We survived everything.

Now, we're back.

Think about that. Your ancestors, your roots, survived all that horror. That is why you're breathing today. You live today because they survived yesterday. And the rule of nature, of evolution, is that the strongest survive and pass their traits along to their progeny. Their suffering and survival are what made it possible for you to exist, and for you to evolve. That means the same strength that flowed through them flows through you.

But here's the catch: You're strong enough to survive all of that...only to work away your life. To these people, you're just a laborer. You're just a worker. You got no name; you got no roots you can trace. Even though you have strength that cannot be matched by those who enslaved you, you still have nothing. The world taught you to have someone else's boot on your throat is normal, all the while you never knew that you have had the power to break that leg like a twig and stand on your own.

You've got nothing until you think like a King, move like a King, declare yourself a King. Declare yourself, give yourself a name, and give some actual meaning to that name. Give yourself some roots. Give yourself and the ones that come after you some heritage, a legacy to follow, because they took that from us, and now we must take it back. I realize that everything that is *us*—and everything that is *for* us, we must suffer and strive if we're going to get it back.

We must earn it.

Sure, it's not fair that you got to work for something that was stolen from you. It's like your boss stealing your car and making you pay him back to get your own damn car. But weaklings whine about unfairness. It is what it is. Don't bitch about what you can't change; overcome it.

Overcome, and take it back. Take that legacy back. And understand, too, you and your legacy has evolved because not only did you get back what was yours, you had to fight for it. And once you've taken it back, earned your kingdom, you must give it back to yourselves, to those that come after us, to our kids and our community and our culture. We must get it back and give it back to ourselves.

Becoming that king or queen you were meant to be starts with your reactions and your own point of view.

Your reactions are the evidence of your views, your vision. If you see yourself as a winner, you carry yourself like a winner. If you see losing around you, and you see yourself just like those around you, you carry yourself in a position preparing for a loss. As a result, you don't seek to win, you plan to lose. Let's face it, losing hurts less if you have never won. Consider that. What you have and embrace in your environment, what you choose to surround yourself with, is your mindset, and if you embrace that losing mindset just because it hurts less, all you're doing is depriving yourself of your capabilities, your qualities, your potential, and your kingdom.

(IR)RELEVANCE

I've come to realize that most of our youth feel so irrelevant in their own mindsets that they hunger for relevance, even if that means dying by the cops, dying by one another, going down in a fiery blaze of glory, just to have ended up with their face on a t-shirt with their name introduced with "In remembrance of..." They just want to be relevant, even if it's just for one or two days, and to have the attention on them, even if it's at their own funeral. That's what I gather from what I see around me. That's my comprehension of what's going on because

I can't fathom another explanation, no other definition, no other way to describe what's going on with them. Why else would someone be willing to die for nothing at all? I believe they're just hungry for relevance, hungry to escape worthlessness, to escape the pain. They seem to simply be waiting to die.

Understand this, though: dying doesn't only mean ceasing to breathe. Dying is when you lose yourself. Succumbing to what the losers around you think you should be, that's dying. Going to prison for some bullshit, that's dying. Losing who you are and what you love because you just want to be known for something, that's dying. And, of course, dying for the pretend shit, that's the ultimate death, because you just died as someone else, and no one will ever know who you really were, or who you could have been.

One of my best friends who teaches with me told me a quote from Ralph Waldo Emerson: "Imitation is Suicide." That sums it up real nice and neat. It's only three words, but it runs deep, all the way to the core. If you're trying to be someone else, all you're doing is killing yourself, and in the process, you're killing the special part that makes you uniquely *relevant*.

Relevance comes from yourself, knowing yourself, knowing where your strengths and weaknesses lie, and using those to make your home, your world, a better place. My friend also gave me another quote from Emerson that ran really damn deep: "The purpose of life is not to be happy. It is to be useful, to be honorable, to be compassionate, to have it make some difference that you have lived and lived well." That, my friends, is how you become a king. It's not by dying for some trumped up, ill-conceived idea of "pride". Pride comes from accomplishing something, earning something, building something, not peacocking. These young cats strut around, not having done shit, but they carry themselves like they're ten feet tall, grape ape, and bulletproof. They beat their chest and dare someone else to look them in the eye. They die just trying to prove that they're savage. And what the fuck is that—savage? All it means is that you can destroy. There's no pride in destruction, not real pride. That kind of pride is an illusion, something the heart grabs to numb the pain of their reality. It may feel real to them, but it's bullshit. And these young men and women, with all that power and strength, die for something that amounts to nothing more than a damn magician's magic trick.

Find that REAL pride. Build something, something real. Build a house for yourself and your family, build a career that you can be proud of, build an education that enables you to make clear and effective choices, build relationships that last a lifetime, build a legacy. Earn your living, earn love and trust and respect, earn your way. Accomplish what no one else before you did and break generational poverty. Help your brothers and sisters, moms, and dads. Be useful, live with honor and integrity, sacrifice for what's right, fight against what's wrong, and be the motherfucking hero. Be a king.

WAR EXISTS IN US

War exists. It exists inside of us by design. If we were created in His image, we must understand, or OVERSTAND, that war went on in Heaven, and that war carried on in Earth. So, there must be a war that exists between or amid our existence because I truly believe that the physical world is only an extension of the spirit or as a reflection of the spirit.

Now, it's natural that we battle with good and evil within ourselves because He created a son of perdition, which is evil, and a son of righteousness, and both sons are the same being; because He says that nothing is created that doesn't come from him, right? So, He's all in all, and that's all. So, He willed into being everything that exists,

He created everything that exists. He created good and evil, so he is both. So, good exists, and evil exists. Those are simple truths. But, if we're created in His image, then we also exist right along with Him, with both good and evil in ourselves. So, I am not what I will be; I am what I will TO be.

With that overstood, it's natural that we battle with ourselves. One side of us wants to do everything right. The other side wants us to live according to our environment. And if your environment is like mine, then your environment is deadly, detrimental. COMPLETELY, completely debilitating, completely horrific, completely destructive. So that's the first thing that you understand about living when you live where I do, where I grew up. The first thing you learn about living is death: how to deal with it, how to avoid it, and how to inflict it. That is survival.

What I'm bringing forward for the rest of the world to see and understand is that when you're from the ghetto, wrong is right. There's no such thing as wrong when you're from the ghetto, when it happens in the ghetto, when your mindset has adopted the plagues, the strategy of the ghetto, the strategy of creating the ghetto by the adversary. Once your mind wraps around that, it's instilled in you that there's nothing wrong with killing your brother, nothing wrong with selling crack. The only things that are considered wrong in the ghetto, the only offenses you really get taken to account for, are raping, molesting, and ratting (snitching). But robbing, killing, selling crack, home invasions, that's all par for the course, normal as a sunrise. That's just surviving. Hell, that shit is called work where we're from. And we didn't create that. People in power, and people behind those in power, strategically created and groomed us to perform in such a manner.

Now, to prove that idea that war lives in us—it exists because we exist, and we must adhere to our existence. It's not just spiritual, or physical, it's downright biological. For example, you must have certain bacteria, certain toxins that exist inside of your body in order to fight off other bacteria. We, from the day we're born, adapt to our environment. From the second we come out of the womb; we must get infected. We must become toxified. We must get sick for our bodies to be able to build the immunities to protect itself. Every day something dies. We have white blood cells that go to war with diseases that come into our bodies. They die, and they must be reconstructed. Other things then must die to build new blood cells. That's what I'm getting at: war is inevitable, within and without us. We will not escape war. It exists among us, just like the air we breathe. But, just like a baby that gets sick and heals comes through stronger with new immunities, the wars we fight inside and outside ourselves make us strong and mighty.

And here's where they fucked up: they created this ghetto, and they made us strong. They made us warriors. They made us deadly. They made us good at killing and dying. I'm talking about the bottom shelf level, fighting nose to nose and eye to eye in the trenches, killing up close and personal. They, the ones in power, they do shit top shelf—they give orders. They order police officers, the military, the alphabet agencies, to do their dirty work. The ones in power never get their hands dirty. They put a security badge on someone like Zimmerman, a punk who started a fight he couldn't finish with a *kid* and had to pull a gun, like a little bitch. When the ones in power try to tighten security, they give the license to kill to the ones they order to enforce it, and then they applaud the killers for doing "a really hard, tough job" when the same damn ones that gave the rent-a-cop a gun and orders created the situation to need one. It's tantamount to clapping for someone standing up when you're the damn one that pushed him over. But those same "powerful" men, those coward motherfuckers cannot, cannot, I repeat, CANNOT face off with the soldiers that they created just to have killed. They strut around like they're untouchable, but that's because they're as fragile as a damn baby bird. There's no way in hell those armchair assholes who grew up walking on gilded floors could stand toe-to-toe and faceoff with someone who grew up surviving the streets. So, the same assholes pay someone else to do it. They must stay united, crowded in a scared mass of affluence and pomposity. Soldiers can stand alone and face the world. Think about that, though: what if the soldiers stood together the same as *they* do?

What separates the creampuff so-called powerful people from the soldiers is a distorted perception of reality. They think they are in control because they have money and influence. Unfortunately, the soldiers think the same thing. But consider this: if the lights went out today, who would make it to next month? Money doesn't count for a thing without civilization, and civilization is man-made. Take that away, and the "civilized" gentlemen wouldn't last a day.

Here's the point—war exists right inside of us, and to survive, to remain healthy, we must be able to embrace and accept death as well as the beauty of life and giving life.

CHA-CHI SIMMONS, CO-WRITER DARRIN CAMPBELL

So, who are you? Do you know yourself? Can you begin to realize the strength that you have? That strength that courses through your veins, that gives you life, what if you directed it towards the light and not the dark? Towards standing shoulder to shoulder instead of nose to nose. Imagine the world we could build, the future we could build. We could do more than just survive. We could live and live well. We could win!

Reflective Questions: This book isn't just for reading. It's for reacting. It's for learning. Consider these questions, answer them for yourself, and write it down. This gives you something to reflect on, something to document where you were so that you can track your progress. Most importantly, though, be honest—brutally honest—with yourself. If you can't be honest with yourself, how the hell could you be true to anyone else?

It's time to get to know yourself a bit better.

12

From where do you draw your strength? What did you suffer through? What wars have you fought (or that you're still fighting)?

_____

_____

_____

_____

_____

_____

_____

_____

_____

_____

_____

_____

_____

What do you want to accomplish? I don't mean be a pro football player or whatever. I mean, what impact do you want to have on this world? What do you think you'll need to do to make that impact?

_____

_____

_____

_____

_____

_____

_____

_____

_____

_____

_____

_____

_____

If someone wrote a dedication to you, what would you want it to say? Read what you wrote here again and again and keep revising it.

_____

_____

_____

_____

_____

_____

_____

_____

_____

_____

_____

_____

_____

_____

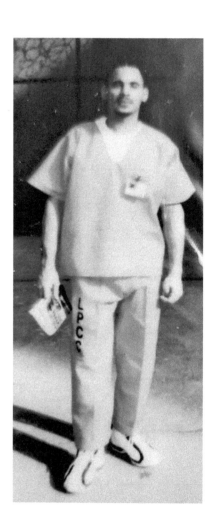

CHAPTER 2

Mistakes

M is-take—an action or judgement that is misguided or wrong

Root word—"take", meaning to lay hold of (something); to reach for and hold

Prefix—"mis" from the Proto-German, meaning "divergent, astray"

Mistakes happen when you reach for something, but you miss. They happen when you try to do something and fail, or it could happen when you reach for the wrong thing and succeed. But mistakes are valuable, and when you approach them correctly, you can always turn a loss into a win.

We all make mistakes, but what defines a mistake can have so many variations. What is a mistake? A mistake is when someone does something against the by-laws of society, a relationship, or one's self. By-laws of society are meant to help you, not hurt; they're intended to establish a natural order and balance. After all, you're supposed to love thy neighbor and work as a unit to conclude or solve a problem. Hell, that's what grown-ups are supposed to do. Anything against that idea, anytime the neighborhood or society is divided, it has the potential to create mistakes.

At least, that's the connotation. That's how most people see it, anyways. It's a mistake to break the law, to argue with your neighbor, to be different.

But really, I don't think that there is a such thing as a mistake. There's no such thing as losing. That's what other people call it, outside looking in, but really, the only difference between winning and losing is how other people see you. How you see you, though, is what's important. Let me clarify that, though: I think that losing is being dumb enough not to know when the mistake you made can be turned into a win. There's really no such thing as losing if you approach it right. You either win, or you learn.

In this light, well, I've learned a lot.

You see, it's my natural instinct to love and to help. I say it's natural because I was never raised. I never had anyone to instill anything in me. No one taught me right from wrong. I had to learn it, instinctively, and put words and meaning to it to become aware of it. I'm a product of my own desires, my own need to feel complete. So, that's who I am: fearless, loving, giving, and the hardest part of 2019 for me was that…

I've witnessed a lot of horror in my life, and I still witness it. I see the youth fall for the tricks, glorifying the monsters and making fun of the saints, seeking entertainment over enlightenment. They become pigs in the blanket, wrapped up with no escape, ready to get devoured by the greedy. Half the youth, maybe even three-quarters of them, will never get to experience fruitfulness and prosperity. So many young trees that get sawed down without ever bearing fruit, never even get to sow roots. It's sad, man, to know that more than 50,000 juveniles are in prison and juvenile jails, here in Amerikkka. They're "raised" in a place engineered to create monsters, and when they act on those monstrous impulses, they're put behind bars to produce free labor. They're sold back into slavery, no rights to be respected, no humanity. No better than livestock.

You don't believe me? It's in the 14th Amendment to the US Constitution, section 1, in the fine print:

> All persons born or naturalized in the United States, and subject to the jurisdiction thereof, are citizens of the United States and of the state wherein they reside. No state shall make or enforce any law which shall abridge the privileges or immunities of citizens of the United States; nor shall any state deprive any person of life, liberty, or property, without due process of law; nor deny to any person within its jurisdiction the equal protection of the laws.

This was drafted in 1866 and ratified July 9, 1868, in the wake of the Civil War. Its intent was to extend the rights granted freed slaves. But look closer— "nor shall any state deprive any person of life, liberty, or property, WITHOUT DUE PROCESS OF LAW..." This gave the State, the government, and those who run it, the power to take your life, your freedom, and everything that you have. Sure, they must follow the laws, but who the fuck do you think writes the damn laws? Same ones charged with enforcing it. Here's the thing about power: those who got it do everything they can to keep it. They seem to show righteousness, but they gave themselves an out, a way to keep control over those they'd enslaved. That, and more, because now anyone and everyone, regardless of skin color, could get enslaved, sent to prison to work for pennies an hour. Why else would a drug dealer often get more jail time than a rapist? It's simple—there's more drug dealers than rapists. That, and the rich fools with politicians in their pockets are the ones who are usually the damn rapists.

But what do you think—is it a mistake to teach my kids to shake hands or shoot a gun, considering all of this?

Well, think about the ones that the lean and the drugs and just the so-called entertainment that killed them. They became my main source of pain in 2019. I see all of this, and I can't live out my person. I can't be me because I can't help. I see people in need on the side of the road, hopeless and desperate, and I can't follow my own damn natural instinct to provide safe harbor because it could mean death. It could be a trap. A woman crying out that her baby can't breathe, that her baby is choking, and when you run to the car or the house or whatever you got to do, only to get cold iron pressed to your head. Just trying to help, and you're dead. You get kidnapped, your organs sold, or you get raped and sold into sex-slavery, all because you decided to be human to another so-called human, only to learn too late you met a wolf in a wooly dress. Hell, man, these kids grew up with Freddy Kruger and Chucky and think that shit is real, that in horror and blood lies the fun, and they try to live it out and emulate the monsters they look up to. And other kids flock to them and want to be just like them.

Think about the prolific amount of mental illness that we're all surrounded by, and consider how many of these mental illnesses go undiagnosed, all the anger and hate that permeates EVERYTHING, from the highest to the lowest, richest and poorest. Just look at the damn president; this is the way the world is going. Cheaters and "reality" TV show hosts get idolized and elevated to the most powerful positions on Earth, and good people get chastised and ridiculed for speaking the truth. It's madness, pure and simple.

So, this is the time when you got to ask yourself if this is the moment for you to fight back. Is this your moment to be the hunter, or the prey? To be honest, sometimes, I don't know where to go for me. I don't even know how to raise my kids. I don't know what to tell them anymore. What advice can I give them about loving and being caring when the reality is that they may fall victim to what's considered fucking normal?

You know what's really sad, though? The same people who are committing all of these horrendous things are usually quoting scripture while they do it, the same scripture that says to love one another, to be charitable, to take care of the poor and the weak, to be human. It's all twisted. The ones who preach the scripture twist it to prey on others. They preach love and humanity to spread hate and monstrosity. They bow their heads in prayer while smirking with their fingers crossed behind their backs. They orchestrate the poor into dog-eat-dog battle arena called the ghetto, turning our young kids into Frankenstein monsters, and those kids' parents throw money and praise the ones who created the monsters. This is the world in which I'm raising my kids.

So, is it my job to teach my children to shoot a gun instead of shake hands? Do I let my kids learn ballet, or do I let them learn karate?

The other day, my kids just wanted to go to the grocery store, and I had to teach them a maneuver to get away from kidnappers. I had to give a long, drawn out scenario about a kidnapper, how to look for kidnappers, how to be aware of their surroundings and hidden dangers. I learned in Angola, the bloodiest prison in the world during its bloodiest time, to grow eyes in the back of my head, and now I'm having to teach the same lessons to my children just so they can be safe at the motherfucking grocery store! By the end of it, they didn't even want to go anymore. Still don't.

Sadly, though, it's not me robbing my kids of their childhood. It's the system. The monster factory that the government set in place is what keeps my babies at home, scared to go out to buy candy. That same system calls me a devil for defending myself against them because I see them for what they are, because I see the unjust "laws" that they try to force down my throat. I'm not choking on that bullshit, and they sure as hell aren't going to try pissing on my head and tell me it's raining. But I had to survive everything that they threw at me already, and I came out punk-less, a King, stronger than any of them ever will be or ever could be. And that's a problem. The one they thought they'd shove around like a baby lamb ended up being a lion in the concrete jungle.

JUST BECAUSE SOMEONE SHOWS YOU THEIR TEETH DOESN'T MEAN THEIR SMILING

I use that phrase a lot when I'm speaking to young people. In nature, every species you see has evolved in order to survive. They evolve to have stripes, spots, certain colors, dangling glowing orbs, all sorts of different types of camouflage and honey traps to lure in their prey. But animals are innocent; people aren't. And nothing, and I mean nothing, can fool you like a human. No other species on Earth goes out of its way to lie, cheat, steal, or kill its own kind the way humans do. And humankind's biggest trap is simple. It's a smile.

Now, that smile doesn't always have to be in the form of an actual smile and showing teeth doesn't always mean showing literal teeth. People can stroke your ego, pat you on the back, pour honey in your ear and whisper sweet nothings to you, try to endear themselves to you however they can. These parasites distract you from recognizing that they're either using you, hindering you, or just benefiting from you. They sell you on the lie that you need them. Worse still, they convince you that you're not you, or that the things you're doing right aren't the right things to do.

Why go to school when you can drop out and make a ton of money selling dope? Why you want to stay faithful to your woman when everybody else is running around? Why are you trying to help those people? These are just a few examples. Most of us have heard some version of those questions. And I bet you hard damn money, when they asked you, they had a big damn smile on their faces.

Whenever a dog, a lion, a tiger, or a bear shows you their teeth, that is not a smile. That's a growl. And what comes right after the growl? The damn bite. Keep that in mind. Let me give you an example.

I remember when I was about 13 years old, and the guy my mom was dating had come over. He was drunk, and I remember this guy had a 1957 Cadillac Coupe Deville, two-door, original gold color, fucking playa-ass whip. It was my dream car.

I remember this guy asking me if I wanted to drive his car, and I was thrilled! Of course, I agreed. I drove the guy's car. I had no idea that this guy's intentions were just to distract me, to get me off my attentiveness, my game, because I'm naturally a protector. I was the man of my family, even at that age, because I was the only man, the only masculine figure surrounded by women. So, naturally, I was going to protect them. All this time this dude was luring me, luring my attention away from my duties.

He showed me his teeth and got me man, drew me in bro, lulled my instincts to sleep, distracted me with a shiny ride. While he had my eyes looking elsewhere, he shot my mom, and he left her paralyzed for life. That's the moment I learned that LIFE LIES.

My whole life since then, I felt like it was my fault that my mom was gunned down. But you get the moral here. This guy showed me his teeth, but he wasn't smiling. He was literally growling at me, and then he bit me, infected my childhood, and impacted my ability to see things clear. Y'all remember, though, that if things seem too good to be true, they probably are. And don't fall for a smile; see past what you are looking at in a person. Eventually, they're going to show you who they really are, and believe it when they do.

DRUGS = PAIN

So, when you're selling drugs, one side of society is eating, and the other is suffering. The obvious consequences of selling drugs, because selling drugs is against the bylaws, is that you go to prison. Now, you're a slave, dead to the world.

Other consequences may not be so obvious. When you get caught, the ones you have been feeding now have to suffer because, majority of the time, the little bit of money that you made selling drugs and (if you weren't just a corner hustler), the money you made you have to spend on attorneys and bail. If you're smart, you saved up a little dough, and now all of that must go on trying to fix or ease the predicament you're in. That's another big mistake, selling that poison in the first place. It isn't damn rocket science for anyone to say that selling drugs is wrong, but when you're divided to the point where you have to feel so alone that you must do what you have to do for you and yours. No education, no job prospects, and food ain't getting no cheaper, how else can you survive? But you never realize, while you think you're helping, you're not. You're hurting your whole community, the whole neighborhood. You never realize that the whole society is you and yours.

Think about this. Let's say you're selling, making decent money. One day, a crackhead comes up begging, desperate for a rock, but he doesn't have any cash. You send him packing. So, he tries to get the money another way. He goes and robs. That person he robs, could be a mother, daughter, grandmother, just another innocent. Could be your family. Hell, he could rob you. One thing's for sure, he robs someone's family. Let's say he gets nervous, that he's got a gun, because let's face it, it's not all that fucking hard to get your hands on some heat. Let's say he shoots.

He kills. You were just trying to do right for you and yours but look at what you did to others. And that pain infects the whole neighborhood, the whole community. Yeah, you may not feel the pain directly, but everyone around you starts to, and it'll make it to you, too. Pain like that, it spreads like a disease, one that no one is immune to. It infects everything, your children, your paralyzed mama. Everything.

RELATIONSHIPS

Now, in a relationship, a mistake is violating the bylaws whether the relationship is family, brother, sister, mom, or dad. Or Friend. Or a group of coworkers. When you have an agreement to love, honor, respect, work as a unit, that's a relationship. If someone violates that agreement, it's a mistake. Before we go further, lets overstand one thing. Division gives power over you, to a system, that devised the formula that created an opportunity for the division.

Let's take marriage, for example. It's intimate. If one of you steps out of that relationship, or lies about something, or keeps something hidden, or even cheats on the other, when that rule is broken, you made the mistake because everyone suffers. The kids, your spouse, the household, your family, everyone suffers because we fall victim to a programmatical standard. This standard that was set up by the entertainment industry, which makes being sneaky or sly look cool. As a result, the unit that you were supposed to care about the most, the one that you invested in the most, the one that invested the most in you, is broken. Everything that you've established now gets divided. Most of it gets lost in the midst of trying to rectify that mistake or suffer the consequences of it. Here, rectifying means getting a divorce so that you don't have to deal with the memories, the headache, and the heartache. Emotionally, you're taxed, you're depleted. Mentally, you're probably suffering all the same. But you must get out. You can't live with someone you can't trust. At the same time, everyone still misses that unity, the family. Imagine, you hurt whenever you see the one you love, or loved, and knowing that they betrayed you. But, at the same time, when you're by yourself, you miss what you always loved about them. Damned if you do, fucked if you don't. Believe me, I've lived it.

Or take friendship. Sure, friends come and go throughout. We change, our goals change, our paths diverge. But that loyalty, that truthfulness that you get from real friends, cannot be underestimated. Friends are family by extension, ones that earn the right to be in your life instead of just being born into it. Real friends tell you truth, no matter how much you don't want to hear it, no matter how much it hurts. I remember telling one of my students this. This boy had everything going for him. He was the damn poster boy of the whole college; job offers from people who have the governor on speed-dial. He was my friend, so I told him that if he didn't commit to getting his education, didn't keep his nose clean, didn't jump on all these opportunities, that he was a damn fool. And, if there was anyone else in his life that was telling him different to cut them out, because they weren't his friend. Sad to say, this boy listened to his "friends" instead of me. He could be making six figures, but he's slaving away with everyone else for just over minimum wages. He's learned from his mistake, thankfully, and he's finally realized that I was his true friend the whole time. Friends are the ones who earned the right to piss you off; anyone who's telling you what you want to hear is just another snake in the grass.

Here's the lesson: don't make a promise you can't keep. If you commit, you go all in. So, trust slowly, build the relationship, make sure it has a strong foundation, make damn sure that the ones you choose are the ones you never want to lose. Moreover, don't create a problem trying to fix a problem.

PROGRESS AND AVOIDING ROADBLOCKS

I'm a firm believer in reality. The reality is that we're all in some kind of fight. My philosophy is that, in the middle of a fight, if I can't lift the people up and help them, it's best to stay out of it. For instance, if your car is stalled, you don't need help sitting in park, sitting on the side of the road. You need help moving it. Fights make people stand still, not progress. So, if I can't propel your life, then I stay out of it because I'm not going to assist you in being sedentary, and I'm not going to empower your stagnation. I'm sure as hell not going to break my back pushing your car if you're not trying to pull. I've got places to be. I got things to do. I'm on a mission, and I'm not going to interrupt my mission to help you if you're already at your destination, sitting in park. I'm out to help anyone and everyone, but I can't help someone who refuses to help themselves.

Unfortunately, though, there are some people who make it their mission to keep you from making it to your destination. Think about that word for a second: destination; it has the same root as destiny. It's where you're meant to be. These people, though, they're highwaymen, bandits in the bushes, doing what they can to slow your progress, to stop your path, or divert you into getting lost.

Really, most stagnant people don't realize that they're slowing everyone else down, too, because it takes all of us to make the world go around. It takes the crippled and the blind. It takes the poisonous and the beautiful, the auspicious and the evil, the strong, the weak, the fat the small, the gay, the straight, it takes all of us to make the world go around in every aspect. It's a war between progression and digression. The best thing you can do in this war is choose a side; either choose to be in continuous progression, or you choose to side with continuous digression. I'm too experienced to believe that anyone on this planet can save me from myself, because I'm my only real enemy. Me, because it's up to me to speed up if I'm too slow, to be conscious enough to see through the bullshit, to recognize when people are just hustling, or when people are genuine. You know, though, the same is true for everyone. We're all our own worst enemies. Everything we need to be great, or to be devilish, resides within us.

Now, at this point in my life, I choose to be auspicious. That's a promise that I made that I have no intention of breaking. However, I understand—in fact, I OVERstand—that preserving myself is first and foremost, because if I can't preserve me, if I can't help me, then I can't help you. How could anyone help someone if they can't help themselves? This means that I have no intentions of letting anyone hinder me, take anything from me, hurt me in any form or fashion because I will defend myself, whether that's physically, mentally, or even spiritually. So, with that overstanding, we can know that life is going to be your biggest adversary, which is yourself. Nobody can hit you as hard as life, as yourself.

It's crazy, funny even, that the only thing that you are is the only thing with which you can't fight back. You just keep trying. Maybe you try and fail. You can plop down on your couch and say, "Fuck it, who cares?" Or you can analyze the situation, learn from it, and get your ass off that couch and try again. I already said it: you either win, or you learn. If you don't rise again, if you don't learn anything, you're just being willfully ignorant.

So, the best thing, if you really want to leave your mark on this world, is to develop yourself. For parents, develop your children to see things clearly. Don't lie to them, kids see right through bullshit. Teach them the truth, the reality, so that they can progress themselves with a clear heart and righteous intent without being waylaid by the vultures, and so they don't have to fight against themselves. I always tell my students that the way you start something is the way you finish it. If you start sloppy, you end sloppy; if you start motivated, you end motivated. Nothing's going to change it; it's a natural bylaw, the way the world is built. Always begin with a clear head, clear heart, and fire to excel, and don't let the detours and speed bumps keep you from your destination, your destiny.

Reflective Questions: I know, you probably didn't expect me to keep giving you homework, but if you want to get the most out of this, it behooves you to reflect on what you just read here. So, here we go.

What is the biggest mistake you've ever made? What did you learn from it?

_____

_____

_____

_____

_____

_____

_____

_____

_____

_____

_____

_____

Has anyone ever "smiled" at you only to dick you over later? What did you learn from the experience? Remember, don't get mad, get smart. You may not be able to go back and change things, and quite frankly, revenge shouldn't be in your mind here. You're building you, so extrapolate the lessons that life taught you here.

_____

_____

_____

_____

_____

_____

_____

_____

_____

_____

_____

_____

_____

_____

What relationships are the most important in your life right now? And how have your relationships changed over the years? And, why, do you think, the relationships have changed? Here, consider your family, your friends, your romances. Most importantly, consider yourself and the relationship you have with yourself.

_____

_____

_____

_____

_____

_____

_____

_____

_____

_____

_____

_____

_____

_____

CHAPTER 3

Side Effects of "Mistakes"

We've already talked about mistakes. It's simply a situation that will have a negative side effect in your life or someone else's life. Some side effects are temporary, and some are permanent. Take my situation. I tried to fix my situation, but it was well beyond my control, my personal power. I was old for my years, but I was still a kid. And I did a childish thing. I started selling drugs because my mom got gunned down. Even though we were in dire need, living in squalor and feeling the pains of poverty, selling drugs was a mistake because it was a temporary solution. I was homeless, sleeping on park benches or in the bathroom in the park, alone... a teenager, not knowing what to do. I was misguided, and I had a kid of my own that I had to raise, that I was responsible for. A kid raising a kid. And I was still a boy, and I didn't learn from the first mistake and went and got another girl pregnant. All the while, I was selling drugs, trying to buy my way out of poverty. The mistakes led to other mistakes, toppling like dominoes in a row.

Selling drugs isn't a regular business. You can't call the cops when someone robs this kind of business. It's left to street justice. Needless to say, I ended up shooting a couple of guys in self-defense, killing one of them. That was K-Dog. His name, his face, is etched into my memory, knowing that I took his life. I was warned not to go down that path, not to sell drugs and peddle poison, to fix my problem. But no one can ever fix their problems by making other problems. Now, fast forward 30 years. My daughter, who is in her early 30s, suffers from abandonment issues, mental issues, anger issues, depression. My son, being born while I was in prison, never had a chance to have a positive figure in his life. He went down the same path, learning from his surroundings, listening to the serpents showing him their teeth. In the scripture, Ezekiel chapter 18, in so many words, it says "The sins of the father pass to the son." That's what happened to my son, literally. He got accused of murder, acting in self-defense. He got shot, almost died on the streets, all behind drugs. Same as his daddy.

But I learned from my mistakes. Now, my kids have yet to make their loss a win. Regardless of the stature they have established for themselves at this point, they still associate rectifying a problem with the same lifestyle that caused us so much pain. But they can progress, learn from it, move beyond it, realize the strength that they possess. I don't just believe they can; I know they can. I know they will because now they know they come from royalty.

THE VALLEY OF DECISION

Sometimes the only avenue we have is to traverse the Valley of Decision, where you must cross the deepest rock bottom to choose a path. In general, people choose their own destiny. Their lives' path is dictated by their own decisions. But there are times where you're just in the wrong place at the wrong time. Worse still, sometimes you're in the wrong place, at the wrong time, for the right reasons, and you get caught up in some bullshit, just a mistake of proximity. Still, though, even those that are victims of bad space-time, much of your lifespan, your decisions will determine the outcomes.

I remember reading something back when I was in Angola, a quote that I couldn't quite remember the exact words, but I remember the exact message: There comes a time when every man must face the features of his inner self. Knowing your inner self means knowing what makes you tick, your motivations and goals, your values and beliefs, your purpose in this world. Now, that's the shiny side of that philosophy. Remember, we're all built with capacities for good and evil, so knowing yourself— your WHOLE self—also means to learn how to survive. It means knowing to what depths you will delve to keep breathing, how far you'll take it, how much you're willing to take away from the world to stay on it. That's a scary valley to cross, to not just conjecture, but to KNOW how cruel you can be just to stay alive. But, to survive, and to succeed in this world, you must learn the depths of your own cruelty, and you must learn to fear your own cruelties. When you're walking that Valley of Decision, knowing what's at the bottom helps you find your way out and back to the top.

Decision. Noun form of the verb "to decide." It's derived from Latin, where it literally means "a cutting off." Making a decision means you cut off the other possibilities, where you cut off the other paths, and choose to focus on one in particular. Decision making is a very lucrative process—very tedious, but very rewarding. Making good decisions usually depends on knowing the field, knowing yourself, and knowing generally how to proceed. It takes time, research, education, skill, and guts to make good decisions. Bad decisions usually result from poor planning, going off half-cocked, losing your patience or your motivation. Like I said, you finish something how you started it. Still, while we can often see immediate results of our decisions, like dropping a stone in a pond, sometimes it's hard to see how far the ripples will flow from that decision.

Here's my point: What seems like a good decision now could determine life and death of you and your lineage later. We must be constantly conscious. We must remember that every step needs to be calculated. This life is a giant chess game, especially when you're a person of color, and you must remember that every move sets up the next. So, your mission, your journey, is never over. It's never going to be over, not while you still have life in you. It last forever, and every time you win, that was just a move for the next fight. That was just preparing you, putting you in the right position, giving you strength and substance and endurance for the next fight.

Just like chess, though, one piece doesn't win the match on its own. You must decide on what soldiers you want at your back and at your side, what army you want to be in, the ones you want to go to war with you. Choose wisely. You don't want someone who's willing to sacrifice you just to get ahead.

My same homeboy that keeps feeding in Emerson quotes gave me another one, this one from the Buddha:

"Thoughts become words, words become actions
Actions become habits, habits become character –
Watch your character, for it is your destiny".

Decisions are everything, and they're in everything. You're going to fuck up sometimes-- Learn from it. You're going to win sometimes--Don't take it for granted. Regardless of the outcomes, let your decisions make you stronger, plan your next move, and keep fighting.

PRESSURE CREATES RELIEF

I was hanging out with my homie one time, the one full of random ass quotes, expounding in depth, like we usually do. We were talking about the pain life gives. He spouted off a random movie quote, this one from The Princess Bride. He said, "Life is pain; anyone who says different is selling something."

Man, I know one thing: life can be painful. Stress, bills, being in love, your children rebelling, your parents suffering and dying a slow death by cancer, your kids getting killed in the street. You're addicted to drugs, and you don't even know how you got there. Anyone who's never experienced pain in their lives hasn't experienced anything.

We all know that pain can be mental or physical, psychological, or spiritual. Even the possibility of pain is painful. Pain causes stress, which causes pressure. But, I want you to understand that pressure--no matter how painful, no matter how scary, no matter how much, how obtrusive, how abrasive it is, how horrific it is—is designed to create relief. That is one of the natural laws: pressure creates relief. When a pipe gets over-pressured, it pops a leak, or bursts, or it explodes, depending on how much pressure is piled on. The reaction is proportional to type of pressure and the degree thereof. But we have ways to recognize and measure the pressure in those pipes, and we have steps to control and relieve the pressure to stave off the explosion. It takes some work, but it helps us avoid catastrophe.

From the human standpoint, we have the same damn tools. Sure, we don't have gauges and dials to measure stress, but if we know ourselves, we know how to measure our own stress. Maybe you're smoking more cigarettes than normal, or not sleeping right, or chewing the shit out of your fingernails, whatever. Everybody's got ticks and tocks. But, if you're aware and ready, you can control the explosion. You can guide the explosion. You see, pressure and relief are simple energy transfers. It's another natural law that supersedes pressure and relief: energy is neither created nor destroyed. Relief from pressure occurs when that energy is transferred into another place or state. So, if you guide the pressure, the energy from the explosion, you can channel it into relief points. Just like when they blow things up: it's a controlled explosion to create relief, to create space, to rebuild again.

You see what they do when they want to demolish an old building because they want to rebuild on that property. They bust the foundations, tear down the old walls, clear up all the old bricks and mortar, and start off fresh. We do this with ourselves, too. Think about it. We're in a constant state of construction and renovation within and without ourselves. When we're at our worst, at the bottom of the valley, we need to demolish the old buildings and rebuild ourselves. You are your physical property. You come from the earth, created from the earth, from the dust of the ground. So, sometimes you have to burst to vacate. You must tear down those walls of poisonous thoughts that have caged you in, get rid of those sinful ways, and regenerate and reconstruct yourself, from the ground up.

Pressure makes you realize that you need to rebuild yourself, that you must make space for the renovation, but only consciousness allows you to realize when or what needs to be done. Awareness. Overstanding. In these you find the power of rebuilding... of rebirth.

But, if you're just floating through life like a damn turd that won't flush, not giving a fuck that you're circling the drain, you're just going to explode. And that's that. You're done. Maybe the anger overpressures, and you shoot someone. You're going to the pen. Or you shoot and someone shoots back. Maybe they shoot straighter than you. Either way, you're dead, out of sight of the world, all that potential in a box or a cage. Be aware or die unaware.

Life is beautiful. I mean it, life is fucking great! I've suffered more than I'd wish on my own worst enemies, and I still see, still know, how wonderful this life is, how beautiful this world and this existence are. Once you start to see what's important, you prioritize, you plan, and you grow. This is when Yahweh starts working in you, and you realize everything that's wrong with you. Of course, that's when stress starts to build again, because you need to feed your family, you need a roof over your head, you need a vehicle, you need a job. You realize that you're in a toxic relationship. That's pressure, once again. It's enough to detonate, to cause a damn nervous nuclear meltdown. Once again, you overstand and control the explosion, get rid of what you can control and manage what you can't get rid of, see reality for what it is and act accordingly, and you continue to renovate.

Don't be afraid of pressure. It's natural. It's going to fucking happen. Fearing pressure is like fearing a sunrise, or death. Fear of the inevitable is pointless. It makes you a slave to fear instead of master of your life. As always, the answer is simple: be brave and handle your fear of pressure, don't give up, and control the explosion. The ability to do this is within everyone. Nothing exists outside of ourselves that allows us to control what is inside of us; everything is within. And when you exercise this kind of control over yourself, you detonate in an entirely new way. You create a spiritual explosion. It eradicates all that poison from those serpents biting into you, eviscerates those influences from human parasites, it wipes clean the soul. All you have to do is reach out to Yah, pray to Yah, ask him to fix you. He'll point out the tools you already have, help you guide your explosion, vacate the old land, and create something.

Yah showed us this way already. He called to Moses to build a house for him on Mt. Sinai, whereupon Moses shattered the tablets of the 10 Commandments. It allowed for a rebirth of His Chosen People, for their culture and their progeny. Understand that YOU, the one reading these words right now, were created in his image. You were built by God to be like God; therefore, you're God. You are God. We all are God. Even in our old body, even with that old poison staining the spirit, you are still God, a son or daughter of righteousness, and one of perdition, of evil.

Understand this, too. Even the Devil is God. I know that sounds a little weird, but I mean exactly what I say. Most people are going to take that wrong, that I'm calling God evil, that I'm worshiping Satan or some shit. I'm not. You know how everyone equates undying, unconditional love with God and inconceivable evil and cruelty with the Devil? Well, what I'm saying is that YOU have the power to be either damn one, or anywhere in between. YOU get to make the decision on where you lie in that spectrum.

I was a devil. I grew up in Hell, so how could I be anything else? I went to prison. I died, in the sense that all my potential, my strength, my purpose, was all caged in a cell. The world turned without me. But I allowed myself to grow when I went to prison. I saw, like really saw, the world as it is. I saw clearly what I'd really done. Yah, He opened my eyes and He made me see the extent of what I've done to my family, to everyone that needed me. He opened my eyes to the pressure, the hunger, fear, the anger. He showed me the effects, the dudes molesting my daughter, the knowledge of my son being born while I was incarcerated, of how he would walk with the same influences as me. Everyone around him is poison. He learned from the streets instead of a father. No Daddy to support him at ball games. Nothing. Well on his way to repeating my mistakes, to perpetuating the pain.

The stress was there. I was ready to die, to feel relevant, to feel any kind of relief. I was mad. I did a lot of crazy things because of all the stress from life, growing up as a youth with nothing. No father, no one to teach me, growing up not understanding a goddamn thing. I got madder. My mama gunned down. Being homeless. Sleeping on park benches. My mom and my brothers and sisters in homeless shelters. It built and it built, and it built. I didn't control it, and I ended up in prison for murder, while in the dope game.

I got to prison, and that stress continued to heap up, like a bunch of fucking devils dogpiling me. Outwardly, I carried myself like a brute, ready to kill or die with no regard to either. Inwardly, I was suffocating, my soul choking. It was crushing me and what I was meant to be. I was the titan Atlas, being slowly crushed by the weight of the world, and I reached out a hand for help. Yahweh took my hand, and He controlled the pressure, helped me control the explosion.

And look at me today. Today, I'm a leader. Today, I'm a king. I'm a college instructor, and I'm about to finish my degree from college. Today, I'm an entrepreneur and personal trainer. My fitness company provides love and help to people. It provides health and, more importantly, longevity. See, controlling the explosion. Today, I'm a community leader. I go back to prisons and provide, teach people how to control the explosion. I sit side by side with the sheriff and chief of police, the same damn ones who would have hunted me in the past, as an equal.

Yahweh showed me the way, how to control the pressure and explosions within myself, and I've marched forward with that gift, spread it among multiple community programs, stamped out smoke before it became fire in multiple community programs and hundreds of lives. I was a taker. Now, I give. I make the world better. That's all any of us can ask for ourselves, in the end. Thank you YAH!

Reflective Questions:

Time for more homework! The previous chapters were really delving into reality and pain, as this one did a bit. But you also read about how life is beautiful, despite all the pain and evil. Here is where we begin the metamorphosis, the change. So, answer me these:

Like I related earlier: thoughts become actions, actions become habits, habits become character. I rebuilt my character by first changing my thought process, which then helped me control my actions, and so forth. It enabled me to harness the pressure for controlled explosions. But, again, you got to know yourself and how you typically explode. Really, this part is of utmost importance, for, as Chinese Philosopher Lau Tzu said, "He who conquers others is strong; He who conquers himself is mighty." What thoughts do you need to control in yourself? And what kind of character do you want to build in yourself?

_____

_____

_____

_____

CHAPTER 4

The Turning Point

I t's important to remember, to harken back to your past, to recollect the pain, suffering, and loss. It's also important to be retrospective, to realize that while you never want to go through those things again, you were damn tough enough to survive them. With this perspective, your past no longer haunts you. Instead, it becomes fuel for your future. You use it to propel and direct your decisions.

If you remember, you're not going to repeat past mistakes. Humans have a notoriously short memory of things, in our own lives and throughout our history. But ask any historian, the purpose of learning History is to avoid repeating the same mistakes. This is true in the big picture, and it's true for our own personal picture. The very definition of insanity is trying the same thing and expecting different results. By that definition, the whole damn world is insane, locked in a self-perpetuating cycle of depression and growth, destruction and rebirth, life, and death. For us, though, breaking from the natural insanity empowers us to break the cycles to which we're accustomed: the cycle of poverty, of crime, of pain and despair. We lug these chains with us, enslaving ourselves, allowing lesser beings to whip us when all we need to do is break out and stand tall. We'll never forget the chains or the scars, and the memory of that pain can keep us going forward, as people and as a community and a race.

I've used the phrase: Listen to your tears. Have a conversation with your tears and your fears. The things that have stressed you, the pains and pressures, the scars, you remember what caused that emotion, and you let that trepidation shape your future. Allow that to make you a more logical decision maker, to prevent the pain from happening again.

My motto remains that you can learn a lot from a dummy, and I'll be damned if I haven't been the dummy more times than I can count. So, learn from me here. The things that pained me were the decisions I made trying to fix my situation. I was poor, so I sold drugs. I wanted love, but fuck, I didn't even know what the hell love was. I fucked up, over and over, perpetuating that street thug cycle, creating more dummies to be just like me on the way.

Now that I'm older, I can see the mistakes clear as day, where they started and how they set off a causal chain that led me here. I went into selling drugs, trying to fix the situation with my family, trying to break away from poverty. I remembered the smell of that public restroom that became my bedroom some nights, the chill of the cold, the pitiful looks other people gave us, the neglect and apathy with which we were treated. I was willing to do anything to get myself and my family out of that. Anything. So, I sold drugs, hard drugs, and lots of them. I got big, cash money raining in. I thought I was a king. Shit, I wasn't any better than a pawn. I say that because, when the shit hit the fan, we lost everything. My "solution" to poverty is what put us right back there. I went to prison, and I ended up abandoning the people whose situations I was supposed to fix. In fact, I left them worse than they were before. That scarred me, haunted me.

I woke up one night in Camp J, sweating cold, and I saw everything clearly. I realized the full extent of what I did, the pain I caused. So, I bettered myself. I transformed myself. I cried and I ached, and prison was horrible, a little slice of the depths of Hell. I used all that anger, all that pain, and all that desperation, and I turned it all into a desperation to consciously fix myself. I still remember and feel that desperation. It's why I'm on the path I am today. It's why I'm a community leader, an educator, an entrepreneur. It's why I'm a mentor and a life coach. It's because I used that pain to fuel my future.

For you reading this, remembering is more important than you realize. You may be getting the hint right now, and you may be afraid to walk again on those stones that led you to agony. Face that fear, and walk it, because tomorrow is still going to come. If you don't find a way to motivate yourself to do the right thing, to preserve yourself, to lay a foundation for your seeds, for the things you're responsible for, then this insane world will find a way for you. For your kids, and those after them, your lineage will only repeat the pain, the confusion, the deprivation, and the same unconsciousness that you did. And now, I understand that's why God used me. That's why Yahweh designed my life the way it was because he knew what his plans were to make a martyr out of me. A martyr, and a disciple. I'm not saying I'm a holy rolling Bible beater, but a disciple. You see, most people just speak the words; disciples live them. Not everyone in this world is Holy, and not everyone wants to be Christian, but no matter our creed or color, everyone needs guidance towards doing the right thing. They need a light to show them the way to righteousness, towards helping one another, toward the last coming first. It can only happen with unity and togetherness. And it takes those who live the teachings to lead the way.

This is your turning point. You, the one reading this. You picked this up for a reason. You're still reading it for a reason. If you've made it this far, follow me a bit more down this rabbit hole, delve into yourself, and OVERSTAND. This is the second that you can choose to change, to be saved. Realize this, know this, and keep going.

Reflective Question: This will be hard on you, but it's important. Remember. What pains have you suffered? What trials have you suffered? What events in your life led you to where you are now? Remember it all, let your own salty tears mix with the ink on this page, and let it all bleed out.

_____

_____

_____

_____

_____

_____

_____

_____

_____

_____

_____

CHAPTER 5

Dummies Save Lives

I don't know how many of you guys reading this are old enough to remember the Crash Test Dummies commercials, where they strapped test dolls inside of cars to crash into walls and other crazy shit. The Dummies even had their own TV show for a bit. They were popular, and for good reason. The test run crashes allowed the auto-engineers to troubleshoot and redesign cars with better safety features, saving hundreds of lives. That, and everyone loves to watch a good car crash. The commercials had a clever saying at the end: "Dummies save lives."

It's true, you know. Dummies do save lives, and not just ones we smash into brick walls. When you lose or make a mistake, big or small, people call you a dummy. Or, you may be innocent, and people who are trying to pull you down, to tear down your spirit or discredit your credentials, they may call you a dummy and try to make everyone else believe it. Either way, everyone wants to be the one laughing at the dummy, not the dummy itself.

Like I said earlier, though, you can learn a lot from being a dummy, from making mistakes. If you approach things with that winning mindset, you learn how not to be a dummy, which means you can teach others how not to be a dummy. To reiterate my point from earlier: I was a dummy, one hell of a dummy. Now, though, I'm one hell of a teacher.

Listen, though, I'm not telling you to be a dummy and do what I did. Being a dummy is okay so long as you learn from it and don't repeat it if you survive it. Nonetheless, deliberately going out to do dumb shit is insanity at its best. The same damn thing that happened to everyone that died on the streets or that got sent upriver will happen to you, if you do the same shit that they did. Learning from others' mistakes doesn't mean trying to learn how not to get caught. For kids that look up to me, I tell them to try to be who I am now, not who I was. Be the savior, not the damn devil.

I'd lost so many damn times that I didn't realize how much I'd actually won, how much I'd learned, until I took a different look at my past. I realized the cyclical pain that selling drugs causes, how nobody ever wins that game. I learned that the streets that raised me weren't the best parents, and that if someone good doesn't teach the kids, that someone or something else will. I learned how to read people, to know the difference between a smile and a growl. I'd always known that, to survive, I'd have to run faster, jump higher, think faster than the next guy. I'd learned that, while that's true, it also deals with the heart of a man, with his true intents and purposes. Everyone has power, has the potential to be powerful; it all depends on how they use it, what they focus on. I'd learned that we're all God, whether you're looking at a super model or a homeless man—we're all created in God's image. These are hard lessons to learn, and no one teaches better than life. Not everyone survives these lessons, though, not when life is teaching. So, I've made it my mission to use my experience, my education, to save others from the same fate. I've been slammed through brick walls so damn many times in my life, I've lost count. I could tell y'all horror stories that would make Freddy and Jason chill out. I've seen what you don't want to. I could have chosen to go that route, to be a monster, but I chose different. I fueled a different path. I'm here to help you learn how to find that path, to fuel your spirit to walk it, and to guide you along the way. That's what a true teacher does: they save people.

ADJUST YOUR GRIP

I've said before that I'm a personal trainer as well as a teacher. Fitness is a huge part of my life because it helps improve and maintain my entire organism. The mind is in the brain, the brain is in the body, so physical health aids mental health and vice versa. This was the subject of much debate in the turn of the century, and the pragmatic philosophers like William James and John Dewey posited the concept of the "body-mind," that instead of the mind and body working separately from each other, that both were just conscious parts of one whole organism. Simply put: strong mind equals stronger body, and stronger body equals stronger mind. You may not be a professional athlete or a Rhodes Scholar, but anyone can improve their own mental and physical health by working on both simultaneously. Working out, pumping iron, all of that, when you let it become part of your life, you realize that the lessons learned from the gym parallel lessons learned in life.

From my experience as a personal trainer, understanding biomechanics and how the body creates movement and balance and how all the parts work together in harmony, I think I finally get what's wrong with the black race.

It's all about the grip.

Here's what I mean: a slight twist of the wrist or elbow or ankle, foot positioning, hand positioning, any minute shift of the body can work a whole different set of muscles, fibers, and tendons. You can feel it if you put your hands on a weight bar. Both hands facing away from you, you can feel your body ready to push. Twist it around to where your palms are facing you, and you can feel your body ready to pull. Twist one hand around to where you got one facing towards you and another away, and you can feel your body ready to twist. What you can do and how you can do it all depends on your grip of the weight.

Now, imagine you don't know how to grip, how to leverage your muscles to move the weight where you want. If you saw someone trying to bench press too much weight, and they're trapped under the bar, what happens if you don't know how to grip and lift? You're more likely to drop the bar on their head and crush their skull, or throw your back into a lifetime of sciatica, than you are to help them.

Your intents were good, but you just ended up hurting them and/or you.

That's what's wrong with the black race, metaphorically speaking. We don't know how to grip each other, to lift each other, and we end up hurting each other. We can trace this back, all the way to Africa. The first Europeans that ventured into Africa didn't exactly give us a good introduction into socializing with a foreign power. We got duped, cheated, used, and abused, and enslaved. Then, we got shipped all over the damn world, our culture and pride and education taken away. Remember, though, if someone good doesn't teach the kids, someone else will. Well, in this case, the captors and enslavers did the educating, or miseducating. We were taught that we're inferior, physically and mentally, that we were beneath those who held the reins and whips, that we needed to worship God as they tell us to, to listen to what they tell us to believe, and if we do, at the end of all the depraved suffering, we could be saved. We were beat with that lie for generations, and we've never healed from the cuts and bruises. We still believe the lie. And we have yet to learn how to lift each other from the ground.

There was one time, not too long after I got out of Angola, where I was flat fucking broke. Homeless, living in my car, starving. Drowning. An old pal from the streets pulled out a trash bag full of legal herb, enough to set my ass back in Angola for another 20 damn years. He offered it to me, to help me get back on my feet, some money in my pocket, some food in my belly. His intentions were good, really. It was all he could do to help. Think about it, though. I may have eaten well that night and slept somewhere warm, but what about the next night? What if I got caught? My friend thought he was throwing me a life preserver to keep me afloat. He might as well have thrown me a fucking gun to blow my own brains out. I remember holding the spice in my hands and at that moment, I dropped to my knees crying to God. Even though my son was hungry and with no other way to feed him, I thanked my homeboy for his generosity, but I declined. Realizing that I was on borrowed time just existing like that, the next day I went to SLCC's welding school to inquire about night classes. When my old welding instructor saw me on campus, he proclaims me the new welding instructor, and here I am to this day keeping a promise to keep young people out of that filthy penitentiary.

I adjusted my grip and pulled myself out of my own black hole. I crossed that Valley of Decision, knew the darkness that dealer's path had, and I found my way.

Our grip, whether mentally, physically, or spiritually, needs to be altered. Some of us, just a slight twist, a slight bend of the elbow, or the knee, or the imagination of the truth, is all we need to push hundreds of years of weight off. This requires overstanding, seeing the big picture, the whole board, so that you know how to make the tough decisions. Like I did: I could have taken the easy route, sold that legal, got back on top of the hustle, because I knew the game well, better than most. But I didn't. I took the hard way, the one that would sustain me, but the one that I would have to suffer for, the one I would have to work harder than ever for, the one that I'd have to sacrifice for. I saw how the righteousness would spread through my sacrifice, how the lives I touched could touch others, how the ripples would roll throughout my home, my community, my family. Every day, we all must choose between what is right or what is easy. Make the right choice.

Reflective Question: You're almost there, now. You've come this far, so let's finish strong. Think on this—was there a time that you helped someone, but it ended up hurting them? Or vice-versa—was there a time that someone helped you, but in the end, it just caused more pain? Write down the narrative, what happened, how did you feel, and what could you have done differently?

_____

_____

_____

_____

_____

_____

_____

_____

_____

_____

_____

_____

CHAPTER 6

Pay Attention to the Shadows

The word "shadow" comes from Old English and Germanic origins, meaning "shade" or "shield", Anglicized into the meaning "to shield from light." Everywhere light touches, shadows appear. If you've taken anything from this so far, it should be to pay attention to the wisdom of the world and what nature shows you. Light illuminates things to help us see, but we, humankind, have survived because we learned to observe what we can't see, to fear the darkness, for that's where predators wait.

Now, as humans and civilization have evolved parallel with one another, people seem to have stopped fearing the shadows. People seem to think that just because the saber-tooth tiger went extinct that they don't have to fear being eaten. What they don't realize is that the game is the same; it's just changed its face.

Paying attention to the shadows means to always seek what's not obvious. It takes practice, experience, education, but anyone that knows how to read the shadows has had to learn how to do it. That means anyone can do it, so long as you work at it.

Let's say that someone is trying to convince you of something. They're going to smile at you, coach their tone to be soothing, try to capitalize on what you fear or what you love. We can see and hear all of that; it's illuminated. But pay attention to the shadows. Listen to what they're not telling you. That's when you'll learn what they don't want you to know. See past what you are looking at, see what they don't want you to see.

Let me give you a story about how I first learned this lesson. I remember my first day on the river (Angola). I just got off the bus with the rest of the inmates, and they shackled us all together and marched us to Camp J. If you don't know about Camp J, ask somebody, and believe the outlandish shit they tell you. The lot of us were shipped off to J for some hopped up disciplinary reasons in the middle of our transition from Hunts Facility. There's no nice penitentiary, but Angola was definitely on another level from Hunts, and to be frank, I was nervous. Hell, I was scared. I mean, I wasn't scared of death, taking it, or dealing it. After all, I learned the extent of my errors. My fears were more transcendental than the rest of the guys I was chained with. I needed to get back home, to my kids, to my paralyzed mom. I needed to get back to the people who needed me. I was afraid I'd have to kill to survive in there, and I knew that if I killed someone in there, I'd never see home again. But I also made a promise to myself and my mom to kill the guy that shot her, and he was in Angola with me, so I thought.

All this weighed on my brain as I walked down the tier. All of a sudden, this guy, one of the trustees who took care of the tier on Camp J, spun out and pushed me. Like, pushed me, not no gentle playground shove. He checked me in the chest like a damn hockey player, and I crashed into the wall. I remember coming off the wall, trying to bounce up like I was spring-loaded, cussing at homeboy for all he was worth, sounding off with all kinds of hero shit like convicts do. My natural reaction was what anyone else's would have been. But homeboy didn't get back in my face or anything. He put his finger in front of his lips and said "Shhhh."

Needless to say, dude had our attention. In a low voice, finger still in front of his lips, he said, "If you motherfuckers want to survive in here, you need to pay attention to the shadows. Pay attention to what you're not supposed to see." He moved his finger and pointed up the hall. "You see that shadow over there?" I glanced in that direction, not really making out anything. "That boy in the cell down there, he got AIDS. He rolls up a magazine, and in there, he got a make-shift needle." In prison, sometimes the guys take paperclips and file them down by scraping them on cement until it makes a point. They use these to do tattoos, mostly. That shadow had different plans, though. "And as we come down the tier, he pokes himself with the needle and puts it in the magazine, loads it up like a fucking dart gun, and he sticks people coming by, just to give them fuckin' AIDS, just because he got it. Just to see you miserable, just to see you die, just because someone did it to him. You understand?"

Someone I didn't know, never met, never did no harm to, tried to kill me slowly with a deadly syndrome, all because someone else gave AIDS to him, but someone else I didn't know, never met, never did any good for, saved my life. The irony isn't lost on me. And the lesson it taught is a part of me. Still until today.

In case I haven't beaten the moral into you yet, let me reiterate: pay attention to your surroundings. Always pay attention to what you're not supposed to see. Pay attention to the tiniest of details, because your life, your children's lives, your survival, your very existence depends on it. In other words, see past what you're looking at. Don't just listen to the words people say. Look through them and hear what they don't say. Listen, and research and learn for yourself. It doesn't matter if it's a gorgeous woman or one of your coolest homies, if they're trying to convince you of something, something that doesn't quite vibe with you, listen harder and hear what they don't say. Always stay woke.

TREES OF LIFE

When I think about how Yahweh says that you will know of me by the things that are made. And remember, you were made, you were created. But then, He says that there is nothing that is created that doesn't come from Him. What I gather from that is that everything I see, even the things I don't see, the things that I can't fathom, all of it comes from Yahweh. It fascinates me bro, just Mother Earth in general. I look up at the trees, and I see Elohim (God). I look at the natural elements, the rocks and wind and water, and I'm in awe of His creations. I'm even fascinated with astrology, how the alignment of the stars and planets and the movements of the cosmos could possibly help shape us. To be fair, I don't know much of shit about astrology, but it still fascinates me that it's an ancient practice, just showing that humankind has always been linked with Mother Nature, to this earth, to all Yahweh's creations. It seems like it's another thing that a lot of us forgot, though.

I've always found peace in the woods, within nature. I especially love walking through the woods, observing the trees. There are some that are standing tall, seeming to reach up into Heaven, so strong that they've weathered hundreds of years of rain and storm and sunshine, robust and healthy, looking like they'll still be standing when my great-grandkids are dead and gone. Then, you see the other trees in their shadows, some of them missing their leaves and bark, pockmarked by woodpeckers and bugs. They cling to life while they rot. It makes me wonder, though. Look at the contrast, the differences between what seems to be immortal and what seems to be waiting to die. Amidst all the beauty and nature, I come to realize that Yahweh created some things for Himself. Some parasites, animals, birds, whatever they are, they were put on this earth to eat the tree, to strip its bark and leaves.

Yet, the tree is still standing. Even though it looks like it's been stripped of everything that keeps it alive, it's still surviving. That means the core of the tree is strong, that the tree is fruitful, and that while it may not look like the neighboring towering giants, that old tree will probably be around long after my grandkids' grandkids turn to dust.

Now, look at humankind, those whom the tree supposedly symbolizes, the palm of our hand, our family tree. Humankind has a symbiotic relationship with trees. We coexist with reciprocal processes to produce energy: photosynthesis and cellular respiration. We breathe in oxygen and take in sugars like glucose, and we breathe out carbon dioxide and let out water. In turn, the tree takes in water and carbon dioxide, and they let out oxygen and glucose. The most basic things that are needed to survive, we give those to each other. But, you see, this is a passive symbiosis. It happens, just like gravity. When we delve to be actively symbiotic, to actively work with the nature around us, that's when real growth happens. My buddy who I keep mentioning grew up in the woods in northern Louisiana, and he told me something an old logger told him, "A managed forest can facilitate more growth and prosperity than Mother Nature can on her own." The loggers make sure the trees aren't crowded up, that they're planted in advantageous places, that they're the right type of tree for the environment, and they take an active role in making sure the trees reach their full growth potential. Man imagine if we could do that with each other.

Relationships like this occur all through nature, organisms depending on other organisms, organisms depending on the earth. Knowing this, seeing this leads you to overstand that Yahweh created people, and people have every tendency of every animal on the planet: every good, every evil, everything. Just as some predators are created with stripes or poison geared towards preying on a certain food source, there are people on this planet who are geared just to eat you. Now, I'm not talking literal cannibals, but these people will take your life. Maybe they eat your money or your things you earned, or maybe they trick your brain and change your personality to serve them, or they stop your momentum to keep you from escaping, or they try to break your intellect and education or manipulate it to work for them. You're losing you, but they're eating and thriving. That's how they eat you, by breaking you down and consuming what they can along the way. They benefit from all your hard work.

It's a sad fact of man, of humankind, that some are designed to be evil, and they know no other way. Others are designed to be pilot fish, lazy fools that pick up the scraps that the sharks leave behind. You could give them the blueprint to success, outline each and every last step they'd need to take, and they'll just smile to your face. They pretend to do something for themselves, all the while they're eating your bark. They'll eat off you if you let them; their job is just to disguise that they're using you. They pat you on the back, feed you pretty words, stroke your ego, capitalize on your good feelings when they tell you all of those awesome things about yourself, all so that you don't realize that they're actually leeching your lifeforce and hindering your growth, weighing down your climb, your ascent to kinghood. Keep that in mind: family, husband, girlfriend, boyfriend, sister, brother, children, friends, strangers, anybody. The human parasite has survived for so long from the kings and queens of the earth because they've evolved to disguise. They look just like everyone else, by design. It's the test that Yahweh laid before us: do you ascend, or do you fall? Will you become a king, or will you become another vulture, a parasite on the Trees of Life?

LEVEL YOUR HOME

As a welder, I love building things. I can see the components separately, can envision how they fit together, can plan the best route in how to put them together, and most importantly, I can see how disparate seemingly unmatched parts, useless on their own, can be composed together into something beautiful, something whose sum is worth much more than all its parts. Building things is another natural movement in the world, as Mother Nature builds mountains and canyons, as birds build nests, as humans build shelters. Everything builds. And, if you study how things are built, you can build yourself into the King you were meant to be. It all starts with the foundation—which is Mind, Body, and Spirit—and strong foundations begin with level ground.

One weekend, our staff from Correxercise, my company, were selling shoes at Jockey Lots just north of Lafayette when my son walked up. It was the first time I'd seen him in 9 years. His mom took him from me when he was only 3 years old. I was raising him, feeding him, teaching him, doing everything that a real father is supposed to do. His mother, on the other hand, was in the darkness. She swam and found herself trapped and drowning in the current of poison that exists in the darkness that usually surrounds places like that, still trying to be Nikki Minaj instead of being a mother. She'd shirk her motherly duties to be on stage. She moved away, leaving me to raise my son. She and I, we couldn't see eye to eye about what we wanted and what we needed in the world. I thought family was life, she thought the show was life. Then, one day, they were gone. I was raising my boy, and she took him, never brought him back to me, instead bringing him into that toxic world in which she wallowed.

I'll give her a fair shake. My foundation was leaning, my ground wasn't level yet. I was still trying to walk the hard path, to do the hard things that were right, to come to terms with the devils of my past. I wasn't the easiest man to be with. So, I can't knock her. No matter how much I wanted to proclaim that I was better than her, truth is, I was probably even more beat up. She had more of an excuse to make mistakes than me because she was younger, less experienced, still believing the smiles instead of hearing the growls. Maybe out of fear, or out of hubris, who knows, she ran from me, taking my son with her. Maybe she thought she was saving him from me. Instead, though, she ended up stealing him away from his protector, and she thrust him into a world of sin and insanity, and for a child, complete confusion. They disappeared from my life. No matter how hard I looked, how hard I pressed, I couldn't find any trace of either of them. I would sit up and imagine his life, picturing the worst. From what I gather, he was abused, mentally and physically, traumatized, maybe even continuing to suffer while you read this. For 8 years, I've been haunted by visions of what may have happened to him, plagued by horror stories of my own telling that starred the same kind of monsters I'd faced.

Then, out of nowhere, while I was selling training shoes, my son walked up to me. Last time I'd seen him he was a toddler, and now he's a 13-year-old young man, grown up from the baby I knew, but I recognized him immediately, as any parent worth a damn would. It took him just a few moments longer to recognize me, but when he heard my voice say, "I'm your Daddy," he knew it was me. He knew that voice that soothed him, who raised him. Tears rushed to his eyes and he buried his head in my chest, arms clasping around me like iron bands, hugging me for dear life. I hugged him back, trying to make up for all the hugs I'd missed. I don't think we moved for like five minutes, barely breathed, afraid it would all go away. He shook in my arms, sobs rocking his body, as I held him up, whispering to him, "I've been looking for you. I never stopped looking for you." It wouldn't have mattered if he passed out, I would have held him up. I was what he needed to stand. A keystone to his foundation.

I was what he'd been needing all those years, what he'd been searching his life for, the piece that he'd been missing. He needed to know and to feel where he came from, what he was built from. Now that I'd completed part of my life's quest, now that I'd leveled my house, Yahweh let him walk back into my house, back into my life. When he looked into my eyes, into me, he saw structure. He saw a King. He saw togetherness. He witnessed my level home, free of bumps and shaky foundations. Up to that point, all he'd seen, in most every person he'd met, was unlevelled and unsure, most wallowing in some kind of self-consuming suffering. He'd witnessed every shade of mental illness, emotional illness, spiritual illness, all the ugliness. He'd been wading through his young life, trying to come to an understanding of all the pain he felt and saw, only finding confusion instead of answers. But in those few minutes, as I held him close, he made sense. He understood that this world is not only suffering and pain, not just sorrow, not just unlevelled homes waiting to crack and crumble. He saw who he comes from, realized the strength that wells within him. Coming from a world of darkness and shadows, he finally saw something bright. And that was me.

Level homes mean strong foundations. If that foundation cracks, if it leans, it starts to cause problems. Doors stick. Cabinets won't stay closed. Concrete starts to crack. The home begins to die a slow death, slowly crumbling. So, correct the problems at the source. Level the foundation.

My message is the same: level yourself for yourself. You see, my son is me. What do you think would have happened if he ran into the old me, the streetcat selling crack? Or the convict in a jumpsuit? I would have been just another damn crack in the wall, something else adding to the destruction of his home, of who he is. That's what happened to me. I sold a rock to this broke down ass guy one time, dude looked like a zombie from Walking Dead, smelled like one too. As he shambled away, one of the older cats form the neighborhood patting me on the shoulder and nodded in the crackhead's direction. "That was your daddy, man." Whatever hope I may have had to be complete, back then, was over. But not for my boy. My home is level. So, when he saw me, he saw the real me. Better still, he saw that he hails from royalty, that his Daddy is a King, that he comes from a king. And best yet, he saw that he himself is a King, that he's destined for great things in this life.

I confess to you, as I confessed to him, I built myself into this level of Kingship so that, should this moment ever take place, just in case I happened to run into him anywhere, that he'd be proud of me. And it came to pass.

So, to you reading this, it's well worth your time to analyze the depths of yourself, to look into your own shadows and see what you may have missed and what you didn't want to see. You need it. More importantly, your children need it. The world needs it. I'm begging you, I'm pleading with you, learn from my mistakes. Level your home before your foundation erupts, before the quakes take it, get right with yourself for yourself, and you'll be right for you and yours.

BUILD YOURSELF

I already said, how you start something is how you finish it. You start sloppy and haphazardly, you're just going to build a mess with more problems than solutions. You carefully plan, work towards perfection, and you'll still come out with some flaws, but you'll construct an excellent home. Any kind of mission, no matter what project, no matter how big or small, takes about ten more times to plan than it does to execute. I don't care if it's hooking up speakers in your car, I don't care if it's a welding project, an essay for school, or putting together a damn Lego set: you have to plan and prepare, or you're going to run into problems, and sometimes those problems can be catastrophic, destroying exactly what you set out to make. The mission of which I speak, though, is of the greatest magnitude. Therefore, your preparation must be careful and meticulous, downright tedious, because you are about to build yourself.

First, you must deeply understand who you are and who you want to be. You've already leveled your home, and you need to plan how to rebuild from the ground up. Everyone's foundation is built upon three primary human aspects: Mind, Body, and Spirit. You can look up the history of any great civilization from around the world: from Asia to Europe, Buddhist Monks to Roman Centurions, from Japanese Samurai to Swahili Warriors, every damn one of them deeply studied and centered philosophical heritage on Mind, Body, and Spirit. Nothing's changed here. People have been people since people began. So, the first step in your planning is to deeply analyze these three keys.

The foundation of the Mind entails knowing your own mental capabilities, limits, and mental health. I know that in school, the smart kids are the ones that get made fun of. Get that bullshit out of your head right now. Not a damn soul that ever walked the earth ever wished to be fucking stupid. You should value intelligence and strive to build it in yourself. You may not grow yourself to be a PhD or a rocket scientist, but no matter who you are and how smart you are, anyone can be more intelligent. This also helps build and maintain your mental health and enhance your own capabilities. The point of learning anything, the very purpose of education, is to learn to think for your own damn self. The fact that you're reading this book is already evidence that you're serious about this aspect; keep it going.

Taking care of your Body should be obvious to everyone but seeing how most people treat their body like rundown amusement parks, I feel the need to be more explicit here. Set a realistic fitness goal, find workouts that you enjoy, and practice self-discipline to stick with the routines. This shit's really simple. If you want to lose weight, then eat less and move more. If you want to bulk up, tailor your diet around protein and muscle builders and lift weights. Some basic research into fitness goes a long way. Also, like I told you earlier, the Mind and Body are intrinsically connected. The Mind is contained in the nervous system, centered on the brain, which is in your body. Therefore, a healthy body contributes to a healthy mind, and vice versa.

Lastly, as the peerless old Karate master Gichin Funakoshi once said, "Spirit first, technique second."

Improving and maintaining your Mind and Body takes training, and most often that training is self-training. So, exercising self-discipline to make yourself workout, to make yourself read a book, to make yourself study, to make yourself eat right, doing all of those difficult-yet-good things build your Spirit, the core of who you really are. You must really think hard about this, meditate on it, study it and write it down: know what kind of Spirit you wish to embody. Everything else in your life will tie to this. Your work ethic, your relationships with your family or significant others, how you treat strangers, everything begins with a level spirit. Seek to build within yourself an indominable spirit, and your entire being will flourish.

Now, you know the home you want to build, the person you want to be. As you move forward, though, don't ignore your experience. If you've connected with this book at all up to this point, you know damn well that we don't live in a perfect world. Therefore, you shouldn't expect a perfect transition. You may level the home, but the ground on which it's built may not be level, and it may not even be possible to level it. So, you must level your foundation with those bumps in mind. You account for how much you'd have to adjust the depth of the foundation to work over those bumps. Do this in your own life. There may be some obstacles around you that you have no control over:

dealers all around when you've got a drug problem, hood rat friends that are still doing hood rat shit, your own shitty reputation that you've built. You can't change what other people do, but you can change how you react to it. Face your fears. Have the self-discipline and strength to say no to the dealer; tell those "friends" that if they're not there to lift you up that they're actually in your fucking way, eating on your bark. Ignore what everyone else says about you because no one knows you better than you. I know that all sounds simple, but I know better than most how hard it really is. Like I said, though, this is the time to choose the right thing over the easy thing. The more you do the right thing, the more times you win against yourself, the stronger you get and the easier it becomes. It's important to remember, too, to give yourself the same amount of love that you would anything else, and please, get the help you need. Research, educate yourself, seek mental and physical health, proceed with a strong spirit that is firmly entrenched in doing what's right.

Remember this, too. Most of us started out with an unlevelled ground. Within and without ourselves, we have high spots and low spots, things we deal with in ourselves and things we deal with around us. Straight up, you're a little uneven right now. You must look at yourself, at your life, prepare for the new renovation of yourself, and figure it the fuck out. Find a way, any damn way, whether it's easy or hard, even if it seems as possible as scraping a mountain to sea level with a dulled shovel, to level your home, to level yourself.

You must start giving yourself the same amount of love that you do everything else. I'm not telling you to say, "Fuck everyone else, I'm getting mine!" I'm not saying to love the bad things you do or have done. But I'm also saying to NOT hate yourself for it either. Come to terms with your demons and learn from them, use them to level yourself out. Be better. That's loving yourself, mentally and physically and spiritually. If those keystones start to wear, though, or if you try to build before those stones are smooth, your home is going to lean. Your foundation, which is the base of you, is going to crack.

Once that foundation cracks in a house, all sorts of problems pop up. Doors won't open or close, windows get stuck, everything jams shut. When the foundation cracks, it's like the house tries to shut itself off from the nourishment and beauty of the outside world. Nothing in, nothing out. The house becomes a prison to itself, stagnant and stale.

I know I'm beating you over the head with this metaphor but bear with me a bit more. The openings we provide, the doors and windows to ourselves, must be in proper working order. We've already discussed watching the shadows, recognizing the difference between teeth and smiles, and all that ties directly to what we let in and out of ourselves, (our lives) and what packages are delivered.

Packages are like blessings, or curses. If your door is jammed shut because your foundation cracked, you can't get the packages inside. Sure, this may protect you from some curses, but you miss all the blessings. It's safe, but it's cowardly. Or the door may be stuck open, impossible to close because your foundation cracked another way. You may be one of those charmed souls whose home only receives blessings—they do exist—but in my experience, being totally open is dangerous. You can't close off toxic friends, toxic relationships, toxic situations. Being totally open leads to bewildered confusion: you can't parse out the bad and the good. Blessings and curses seem to be the same. Point being, you need the ability to open up and the smarts to know when to open, and you simply can't do it if everything within you is stuck.

I want you guys to live a beautiful, healthy, full life. Me, I'm just now reaching the point where I'm levelling off my house so that my doors and windows can work together, can open and close, allow fresh air, some circulation where I can see and feel things clearly, where I can block out all of the toxic memories. Those toxic friends and toxic people, those toxic situations, I can close my doors and windows and be all by myself and the people I love, with the ones that love me. For the first time in my life, mentally, physically, and spiritually, I feel sane. I feel strong. I feel solid. Whole and complete. I give thanks and praises to the most high, and I attempt to be upright in everything that I set out to do. In my life, I put everything and everyone I care about before myself. But, I could have never, would have never, been able to do what I do if I hadn't started with myself. I wouldn't be able to teach, to level other people out if I didn't level out my own house. I wouldn't have the power and influence to help others. Levelling my home, myself, is what equipped me to become an instructor to individuals who are caught up in this technological age, where technology is teaching our children that poison is good. That doing dumb shit with a smart phone for attention is good. That eating fucking laundry detergent will get you famous. That dumping a bucket of ice on your head is good for the world. Or more importantly, young people committing suicide, literal or through imitation, for "likes." Our young ones, the future of our world, is bombarded with poison at a rate never dreamt of.

I must be the reasoning between all that corruption. I must be THE example to the young ones, that they can still be worthwhile, that they can be respected, that they can still be dominant, all without putting it on Twitter. I teach that they can be whole and complete when doing the right thing, and they don't have to post it on Facebook or Instagram. It's kind of hard for them to grasp, that the internet is virtual reality. It's not fucking real. But every time my students or my community sees me, I am sane and comfortable in my own skin with my same respect, with the same credibility as when I ruled the streets. They see that I'm respected for what I was, that I have the ability to die, the ability to kill. They see that I have no doubts of myself or my own capabilities. But they also see me as a living example that you can't go on living like that and still be fruitful. Further, and bigger than that, they see that no matter how deep they sink, they can rise above and ascend. I have respect when I walk through the streets. I have respect when I walk into corporations, when I work on committees. I walk among millionaires and preachers, among the homeless and the helpless, among the evil people and the righteous. And they all respect me equally.

No matter where I walk, I get respect. It's not because I demand it. It's because I have obviously been through some shit, but I levelled my house. Everyone that witnesses me, that really looks at me, knows that I am everything—I'm good, I've been evil, I've been lost, I've looked into the abyss, and it looked back. I found Yahweh, I found myself, and I'm teaching everyone that you must travel that void to find your way. For Yahweh, He existed in a shapeless void in the dark, yet from it, He created everything. You're walking the darkness now, where everything seems shapeless, where confusion and insanity seem normal, but guess what, Yahweh exists in that dark and you must go there to find him. Level yourself. Level your house, level your ground. You come from the ground, you are the ground, you are your foundation, you are your home. Level yourself out. Then get to rebuilding.

Planning Time: Here, we're not just reflecting and thinking. It's time for action. But, like I said, before you embark on this journey to build yourself, you must plan meticulously. First, investigate the shadows of your life, of your environment, of the people in hour life, including yourself. Now, what do you see in those shadows? What traps do you need to be aware of so that you can avoid them?

_____

_____

_____

_____

_____

_____

_____

_____

_____

_____

_____

_____

Phase two planning: you need to level yourself and build a foundation based on the three main components— Mind, Body, and Spirit. Step by step here: What can you do to improve your mind and mental health? Do some research and reflect on what you learned here. Also, how will you improve your physical health? Set realistic goals. You don't need to bulk up like Arnold Swarzenegger or run like Usain Bolt; just be healthy. Lastly, what kind of Spirit, what kind of character and person, do you want to embody? Follow the advice of hundreds of years of wise men and women, and think on this deeply, and write it down here.

_____

_____

_____

_____

_____

_____

_____

_____

CHAPTER 7

Remain Upright

You made it this far. You know yourself, all of yourself. You've leveled yourself, built your foundation for yourself. Now, it's time to get your home built, and it's time to keep it standing.

LISTEN TO YOUR TEARS

Too many people are ashamed of crying. They make fun of you for crying, call you a little bitch, call you childish, call you weak, all because you had the courage to feel something strong, and you reacted to it. They make light of your pain because, in truth, they're afraid of going through whatever you're going through. As you rebuild, as you change, there's going to be tears.

Think about a fat kid who's trying to jog around the neighborhood. His belly is flapping, thigh fat slapping together, he's wheezing for air, turning red. I bet some of you laughed when you pictured that in your head. You may have even made a joke that he'd be moving faster if there was a goddamn cupcake at the end of the road. You know, though, that kid is just trying to change. He's trying to be fit, to be better. But every damn one of his neighbors are sitting in lawn chairs, laughing.

Think about that girl in the neighborhood that everyone's hooked up with, the one that dresses provocatively, the one everyone calls a slut. Imagine that girl putting on some nice clothes, dialing back the makeup. She stops going to parties and starts going to church. She stops skipping school and starts studying. You know how many people are still going to call her a slut? How many people are still going to treat her like a whore? How many dudes are going to keep bragging about how they fucked her one night?

Think about that dude in the neighborhood that just got back from jail. He'd run the streets, sold drugs, got into more fights than anyone could count, killed some people. He's the one that said he'd never leave the streets, never turn his back on the 'hood. Now, though, he's in trade school. Instead of slinging rocks, he's slinging a book bag over his shoulder. Instead of hopping in a car with his homies to go smoke a blunt, he's hobo hopping on a train to make it to class. He's making a life for himself. How many of those "homies" call him a punk now? How many people call him a sellout? How many people say that he thinks he's better than everyone else? How many people denigrate him for trying to change?

Do you think any of those people cried?

Did you know, though, that tears are just a natural bodily response to an excess of emotion. The area of our brain that processes emotions is linked to our tear ducts, and when that region gets over-burdened, our body releases the pressure through an emotional explosion. Hence, we cry.

So, when I say listen to your tears, I'm telling you to try and understand why your emotions got so elevated. Like that fat kid: he's crying because he's embarrassed of what other people think of him. But damn, he's doing the right thing! You don't wanna be fat? Go exercise. But for him, he can get the added mental benefits. He builds emotional strength and endurance, and he strengthens his own capabilities of handling others' hateful bile in a logical way. Those hecklers lost, and that boy won. Just like that poor girl trying to re-invent herself. Those others want her to still be a slut because they think they're better than her. They want her to be low because that makes them feel better about themselves. They tell her she can't change because they're afraid that they can't change. But man, if she does succeed, if she does rebuild herself, imagine how many tears her haters are going to shed.

That last example, that's me. I did that. I was up before the sun thought about peeking out, jumping a train, walking, or hitching a ride 15 to 20 miles. Rain or shine, I did it all because I didn't have a ride, all of that just to make it to shop before class. There were times my teacher found me sleeping outside the shop doors. I poured everything I had into learning my trade so that I never had to go back to what I used to do. I cried, man. I cried a lot. But I listened to those tears, processed what they meant, learned from them. For some people outside looking in, they probably thought that I had come from prison a simpering little punk. They didn't realize that I was crowning myself a king.

Don't let anyone convince you that just because you're an ex-con that you're worthless, that you're a pimple on the ass of society. You've got the ability to contribute to this world, to make it better, to live a life worth living. Now, if you haven't learned anything from your time behind bars, whether it be pain and suffering or actual penitentiary, especially after reading this book, man just get the fuck on with the bullshit. You're being willfully ignorant if you haven't learned from that pain. If you've listened to your tears, listened to your fears, to your anger, your anxieties, your discomforts, your pain...well, then, you would be just like me. The image of God. Lion stout.

What you would be doing is diminishing the danger ratio everywhere that you exist. You would change for the better, which would make the next person better, and the next and the next. Just like evil spreads like cancer, good can spread like sunshine, each of our lights adding to the brightness. You know, I know all of this because I was in prison. Because of what I am now, other people's children are safer. Other people's wives and husbands, moms and dads, friends and grandchildren, everyone that breezes through my existence, is safer. The foundation that I've built for myself doesn't make room for destruction, deprivation, or neglect. Death used to be my fucking roommate, and now I won't even deal with him. I'm not afraid of death, but he doesn't have a place in my world. Life, that's what I'm here for.

I died when I went to prison. Who I was, who I would have been, died in those cold, concrete walls. I died so that I could live, so that we could live.

Be upright and righteous in everything that you do. Be as upright as possible, same as I do. I live my life like Yahshua (Jesus Christ), willing to sacrifice myself for those I love and for what I believe in. I am a hero to the poor and downtrodden, an enemy to the vultures and cancers of the world. I was built to be a slayer or a savior. I was equally equipped to be either one. I chose my side. Now, it's your turn.

No more reflection, no more planning right now. I sincerely hope that you've taken the lessons I've put forward here seriously. Whether or not you relate to the environment from which I hail, I hope you've opened and expanded your heart to others that are different from you. If you did connect with me and where I come from, I hope you see that there is hope, that the misery that you see isn't all there is. There is life and beauty. There is salvation, for anyone and everyone. Here, I want you to make a commitment. Make a contract with yourself. Choose the big thing, the biggest thing, that you will change and/or improve about yourself. Write it down, and stick to it. Remember, in this life, the only one stopping you from earning your crown is you.

_____

_____

_____

_____

_____

_____

_____

_____

_____

_____

_____

_____

_____

_____

_____

_____

MESSAGE TO THE READERS, AND FUTURE KINGS

T o my boy, to Macho, you're going to read this book someday, and I want you to know that I love you enough to tear through all the obstacles, unlearning everything that I'd learned through surviving, to denounce everything that everyone had taught me. Even teachings from my mama, denounced. No matter where it came from, no matter if I got to go against every grain that existed, I unlearned. I leveled myself. I love you enough to happily suffer through all of it. I did it to be there for you, but more, I did it so that you could witness your power, witness your regal bearing, your heart, the sacred blood that runs through our veins. All my kids: Shana, Marquis, my little grownup Brooklyn, my precious Oriyah, my beautiful Alex. Oh, my lovely babies. I love all of you so much, and I've fixed me. I put every bit of the best effort I had, every last grainy spec that Yahweh gave me, into fixing me, all so that you all know that you're Kings. Even the girls, you are all Kings. To be a queen after the suffering you all went through would be setting the bar too low. None of you are second to anyone.

It's kind of repugnant to think of what you're capable of. You see, power is just power, it's not good nor evil. It all depends on where you aim it. All of us, though, we were born with a heart that cares, one that sees the evil around them and one that yearns to help defeat that evil. I already said to you, my babies, that you get that from me. I get that from your grandmother. You got that same kind of power she had. She had the strength to take bullets to prove she was a King. She was the mother and the father, both man and woman, raising eight children by herself, fighting, scratching, whatever it took. She took bullets willingly, still lived 30 years past that. She fought until Yahweh finally took pity on her and gave her relief. We sent her away all in white in a horse drawn carriage, a funeral parade fit for a King. Let's not denounce all she suffered, for you know through me, through yourself, you are all Kings, all of you. I love you all.

Voice of the Experienced

Right on Crime Panelist

Community Leader

Keynote Speaker at Delgado College Convocation

Agent of Positive Change

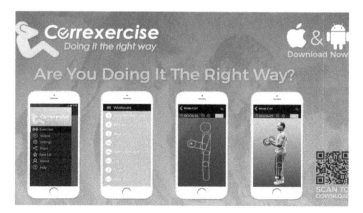

Co-Founder
"Self-preservation equals longevity"

Printed in the USA
CPSIA information can be obtained
at www.ICGtesting.com
LVHW090949060424
776645LV00032B/267